KNOTS

THE HUGH MACLENNAN POETRY SERIES

Editors: Allan Hepburn and Carolyn Smart

TITLES IN THE SERIES

Knots

Edward Carson

McGill-Queen's University Press
Montreal & Kingston • London • Chicago

ISBN 978-0-7735-4767-4 (paper)
ISBN 978-0-7735-9956-7 (ePDF)
ISBN 978-0-7735-9957-4 (ePUB)

Legal deposit second quarter 2016
Bibliothèque nationale du Québec

Printed in Canada on acid-free paper that is 100% ancient forest
free (100% post-consumer recycled), processed chlorine free

McGill-Queen's University Press acknowledges the support of the
Canada Council for the Arts for our publishing program. We also
acknowledge the financial support of the Government of Canada
through the Canada Book Fund for our publishing activities.

Library and Archives Canada Cataloguing in Publication

Carson, Edward, 1948–, author
  Knots / Edward Carson.

  (Hugh MacLennan poetry series)
  Poems.
  Issued in print and electronic formats.
  ISBN 978-0-7735-4767-4 (paper). –
  ISBN 978-0-7735-9956-7 (ePDF). –
  ISBN 978-0-7735-9957-4 (ePUB)

  I. Title. II. Series: Hugh MacLennan poetry series

PS8555.A7724K66 2016   C811'.54   C2016-902130-0
                                        C2016-902131-9

This book was typeset by Interscript in 9.5/13 New Baskerville.

For Joyce, Lindsay, Matt, Mark,
Clara, Graydon & Vivian

If a knot is to yield, the mind must first yield to the knot

CONTENTS

FLIGHT OF THE MIND & MEASURES
OF THE STARS

KNOT THEORY

The mind is made
of pleasures and

uncertainty, inviting
as it yearns to be both
puzzle and adversity.

Far more promising
than loving or belief,
its trust is yet unclear,

unseen, fashioned as it
is to hide the problem
of unravelling. Though
rarely yielding easily,
the mind is not what
you expect, nor what

it might appear to be.
Emerging out of neither
calm nor flexibility, it

lives inside a tangled
coil of still restraint
and true adaptability,

its heart a home of
unforeseen complexity.

Solitary in your thinking,
you are less than many

though rarely alone.
An intimation of love
glides into your head.

It is a tendency without
the rationale of intent.
A fictitious intrusion

of quiet deceit, it is
as if one bird flying by
is also a fabrication,
all the more likely to
arrive fully realized,
much like the thought.

Before you know it
one bird flying by
is nearly impossible

to ignore, difficult at
best to resist, never
mind regret the near

substance of its passing,
the insistence of its cry.

ALLOW A BABBLING BIRD
(for Jay Macpherson)

There is   something   to be said
    about   an Ark

full   of the Kingdom's   few –
    how   faith converts

the serpent's   will,
    repenting or

believing,   unsure   still,
    or balancing   in reason's

blinking   eye   a clear   belief
    in everlasting   clues.

So   welcome   home   faith
    flying   like   a bird

    against the   wind,
then turning   to its perch   in prayer.

Be thou   this silent   truth
    that you   may see,

that you   alone   will say   what is
    not   known   to be.

DEGAS'S PETITE DANSEUSE

Her first   and last
    stride   always

        a step away,
hovering

    as if in flight,
she must be   patiently

  waiting,   one foot
 still   in the past,

the other poised   longingly
    on the edge

  of anticipation.   She does
not   reach for

    the air   above her,
 but gathers it   behind,

her arms'   and body's   curves
   concealing   the shape

    and limits
of her expectation.   We are pulled

to her   like the future,
   all light

on   a familiar   likeness,
  though   nothing

                      holds back
this intimate   proximity

          this persistent
progress   toward solitude.

What appearance proves
its opposite of opposite?

Resisting a much deeper
interpretation, we think
what we know, seeing

the apparent float free
of itself. We consider
what we never knew,

coming together as if
a ready fidelity were
both easy and abiding.
Doubt and expectation
of this view hover
before us, fly readily

into the air as if gravity
alone could never hold.
We wait for something

to happen, the prospect
of what comes next
filling our eyes, the last

of likeness returning
full tilt through the glass.

DESIRE FLYING BY

What desire escapes our
notice, its need being less

apparent than evocative?
Forsaking what is neither
suggestive nor revealing,

we anticipate love, yet
resist each connecting
thought as if it were in

opposition to our heart.
In this, desire is neither
material nor ephemeral,
being far more evident in
expectation than fleeting
in configuration. So it is

that love's covert capacity,
being everywhere uncertain,
is likewise contrary to what is

meant to be. Such ambiguity
fills our lives with the latent
evidence of brief passing,

a restlessness of transitory
thought recklessly abandoned.

Uncoupled   from its solitary
    spin,   this brightest   star

unwraps   the shades   of night.
        In its   whirling

wisdom   we will   trust,
    pleased   as we are   at being

     pleased   inside   the light
of our own   contemplation.

A wary   measure   rides within
      this view,   a cautious

marriage   of what it is   that makes
     resolve   from our belief.

      Into   this common
shine   our covenant   is fixed.

And so   let heaven's   revelation
       be as   it appears,

      positioned   as we are
against   its right   persuasion.

No bright   counsel is   too wise
   to withhold, or too   fleeting

           to deflect.   Welcome, then
to each   new orbit   of our love,

                             '
foreseeing   in this   greeting   sky
           a true   reflection

of what   lets   go   the night,
   these swirls   of light   all   filled

with the pleasure,   the unsatisfied
           present   of the mind.

CHAGALL, AFTER HALLEY'S COMET

Starlight   steals   across   the sky.
   Fiddles   or fish   soar   or sink,

   hovering alive inside the night.
What is   left out   is far   far

less predictable   than couples
   flying   motionless   in a slip

      of air, or pairs of lovers
congealed   in   buoyant   light

circling   the contrary   moon.
   Love   must   resist

   this abstraction   of knowing
another, must weather the itinerant

   touch of desire,   much as
the total   embrace   of the dark

blue   sky   resists   its own
         interpretation.

The virtue   of floating   free
         shines   a light   on

what   is confined,   knowing
         the blackest   blue

of nights   is realized   within
         a human   canvas,

the comet,   like loose   radiance
    reaching   out   to the bride.

This composite   of night,
surrendering   what   sleeps,

calls   together   satellites,
                    gravity

stirring   us away   from flight.
       Whatever   appears

consents   to sun   and stars,
             their   crossing

marking   time,   a luminous,
                    diversion

in trees,   assuming   in us
          continuous   sky.

Diving into it,   proximity
                    measures

our orbit   of belief,   augurs all
     that might be   memory.

This elegant   cosmology
          moves us   closer

to whatever   carries   us
          further   away.

Accustomed   as we are
        to a marriage

of passing   signs, we covet   most
        what   travels

through   this curve   of space,
        wakes   us into

comprehension,   light   alive
        assaulting   everything.

HALLEY'S COMET AS SEEN BY GIOTTO

Everything   is seen   as possible,
        even   composed

as a message   in this light,
        its painted   evening

    sky   flawlessly   expanding
in turbulence,   a disturbance

wearing away   at heaven's eye.
            This soaring

apparition   is on a longer   loop,
    its   telltale   light

        repeating   itself.
Shaking   with   sparks,

    it gracefully   erupts
            with   the after-glow

of fireflies.   Each appearance
        becomes   no   part of us,

though   our   thinking   has
        a way   of teetering

into   the terrain
        of unbroken   belief.

Of celestial   mechanics
          or multiplying   prophesies

confronting us,   the prevailing
          wisdom,

is a climate   of thought
          asking   of our   love

    no   more
than   reason   might bear.

It takes the addition
of one, times the value

of the other, and often
more than hyperbole
to signify, or maybe

multiply the myriad
ways we complicate
the embroidery of love.

Its embellishments reside
between a widespread
scope and rife capacity,
whereas its exaggeration
makes ample room for more
than undue possibilities.

Our common sense says,
love will come and go
where enthusiasm finds

a home; if conditions shift,
we modify accordingly,
amplifying all we've learned

to suit the heartfelt thoughts,
and not the insufficient facts.

Its lasting   purpose   is to
      distract   the eye,

   highlighting   a single
bird   on mountaintop

     or white   village   roof.
Its   borders   are   wider

     than fields   filled
with   snow   and closer   than

     this band   of hunters
forever   marching   home.

   No one   is looking   up.

With   every   head   looking
       down,

     appearing   out
of nowhere,   the men

   just   returning
have no   faces to speak of.

BLACKBIRDS MUST BE FLYING

Not to be   contrary   but in
   the tempting   fall light

of the mindful   maples
     and gathering   pines,

the foolish   blackbirds   exhibit
   an alluring   spray

    of dark   neon blue
splashed   along   their ample

    wings.   This in itself
is not   surprising,

nor is   the intimate   order
   of their   hunting

and pecking,   until that moment
     when,

impulsive   in the hasty   wind,
      they rise,

abandoning   the trees   altogether,
   swarming   into

a sympathetic   cloud,   a diving
     thought,

perhaps,   interrupting
                the sky

    with the idea   they might
yet   behave

    differently,   if only
            they could

think   of an irresistible
                        reason.

LANDSCAPE WITH THE FALL OF ICARUS

A bird's   elusive   shadow
       breaks   away
          from   the sun,
its voice   falling,
       filling   the air,
leaving   behind
       the singular
ambition   of its crossing.

For all   its resolve,
    in the seconds   to come,
there never   will be
     a time or   place
when   it is not   still
    falling.
What this   sustains   turns loose
   a darker . shade,

       tumbling
through   our mind,
    as if   what
happens   next
    could be   an accident
   . of will.
Here   the wide   mouth
  of the sea   swallows
    this act
of retribution,   bringing
       to light

the reasoning   of what
              can't be
reversed,   of what
              can't be
seen   coming   and going.

ORANGE STILL LIFE

At dusk the colour orange marries
        a sense of rest and release,

a continuous   adaptation   arriving
        between   the amber   dawn
and ruby red of the setting   sun.

    Oranges   in a bowl   might also
        wish   to fashion   themselves

after   orange,   knowing   the one
will   flourish   in   transformation
        while   the other   ripens   in

disintegration.   Likewise   this love
        of ours is a   contrary

        condition,   a momentum
that   never   will   be   made   still.
Appearing in this   last light of day

        it   pauses for no   one,
provoking   a likeness of pleasure.

    So   it is   a love   like   this
        in   the   unquiet   dusk
is different from   the morning   air,

    one a tart taste of persistence,
the other a suspension of opposites.

LOOKING FOR LOVE

Arising in the mind,
this simple tenacious

pleasure of detection
sets us free to look for
each object of our love.

By way of recognition,
and though unmoving
or even relocating, our

love is soon revealed
(how near and how far,
how close to or where?)
as central to our thought.
This oscillation of love's
presence knows no reach

it cannot hold, no limit to
its brink. Maintained and
daily modified, our love

is laid bare to re-discovery,
to the mercy of returning
tides where each likeness

rides a nervous wave wider
than direction or reflection.

HESITATION

When   intimacy   multiplies,
   hesitation   steps in,

never too sure   of its rationale
        or reach.

To be   certain,
    each of us   embraces it

    as familiar,   elastic,
wishing for   repetition.

   At this convergence
of proximity,   a determined

enthusiasm,   resilience
        plays out.

Pleasure   is remembered,
   or surrendered,

   while love's   provocation
is both motive   and complaint.

The ready   mind craves   more
    than   this embrace

whereas   the heart   is far
   far away

                from itself,   filling
     an emptiness,   perplexed

by the joy,   the oblique
                distance

and hidden   anticipation
          of ordinary expectation.

A BIGGER PICTURE

Presuming   that two
            birds   flying

east   or west
        is what

                appears
when   the unbroken

line   of their
                    whereabouts

becomes   clearly
                visible   in

        the retreating   light,
this sets   in motion

            the thought
of two   birds

            advancing
east   or west

            who aren't
what   they are

        but what
they   might   appear

to be.
Together   their continuous

          flight
liberates   all manner

          of meaning
as   this image

of two   birds
                         emerging

expands   into whatever
          else

might   spring
                         to mind.

Together   they become
          the vanishing

point   of a thought
          that knows

          nothing
of itself   but knows

with certainty
          that two   birds

flying   east   or
          west

                    is a motion
that moves   us away

            from   ourselves
to something   quite

                            separate,
        something

the evening   sky   daily
            paints   across

                its casually
departing   self.

ONE IS THE OTHER

The river   wraps
            its way around

            each bend,   continues
to flow,

            though   never
                    depending

on the same   solution
            it finds   a place

        to slow   and rest,
                then   flows

            once   more   tilting
forward   into

the shivering   white   cataract
        and sulphur

                            blue pools.
The river   is thick

                with   he satisfaction
of thought,

            enveloping
                    yet   still

unyielding
            not   knowing

        either itself
                    or the challenge .

of its destination.
                    The pull

of the mind   assumes
            this shape,

            knows   tself
to be   something

                            other
than shape,   knows

            itself
as something   appearing

            to modify
all intention.

        A familiarity
like this,   so elastic,

        resists
            all efforts

to remain   in the mind,
            will rise

and fall,   fill and
          empty its own

               elaboration
      of thought

like water   in the contrary
     order of things.

The mind   letting   go
        of itself

is an intimacy   setting itself
           free,

  escaping   like cool water
        letting

               itself go
over rock and weed.

                 Within
this sway,   it's love

      we'll choose.   In this,
holding   fast

     to one   and   the other
means   more

     than we   can know,
       will alter

how this love   of ours
                    emerges

      as a thought,
in part   unconscious

        of the other,
in part   an answer,

      wider than
the water   answering itself.

AUTUMN IN LOVE

Where   all   lovers
    have   a weakness

and worry   what   misleads,
                  autumn

in love   doubts   not   what
    true   love

        might deceive,   being
inclined

    to the tension
             of anticipation

and commotion
              of release.

    Like a sparrow
of thought   hovering

    inside   the mind,
all love

    leaves   a mark.
Likewise   each   thought

    lingers,
nourishing   as an interval,

               practical
as patience.   Autumn

in love   calls   to mind
          a true

                    likeness   of falling
away,

          will let loose   sallow
                    leaves to

confront   the earth   rising up.
                    Riding

in the twirl   and camber
                    drift

and meander   of the wind,
                                        love

has   no motive,   as does
          the wherefore

                    of the mind
which sets free   the raw

pleasure of branch,   the creak
                    and swell

swoop and flurry   of thought.
                    Abundant

leaves   in autumn
        are the temptation

and reason   of a season
            absorbing

                    itself,
whereas   a confusion

            of leaves
is the hiss   of twig and clatter

of swirling,   thrumming bough.
        The mind

creates   this array of abundance,
        filling

its hours   with shadows
            and light,

while love rests   attentive, willing
            as a pause,

subtle   as caution.   A season
        like this

            will   set free
our every   thought,

                        the restless
mark   of a mind
        departing   itself.

The leaves   of autumn
                waver,

ever longing   to remain,
                filling

                        the heart
with a restless   resolve.

                        An expectation
        of preference

looks   far   more
        like a profusion

                        of difference.
Leaves   weather

                into   an uncertain
momentum

and exaggerate   the momentary
                confidence

of their falling.   Wherever
                each

one   alights,   it too
                will delay,

modifying   its flight
                from retreat

to inclination,   hesitation
        to readiness.

                  If autumn
could speak

      it would say   one thing
in love

      leads   to another.
What falls   away

is always   the onset
      to the next,

           a like wind
   passing on

to a possibility
      of common purpose.

LOVERS

Two rivers   brimming,
          waves

          overcoming
                    their shores,   adapt

and rearrange
                    themselves

in the mind,   a necessary
          flow

          for every bend
                    and straightaway

alternately
          breaking

                              ground,
          a course

often   knowingly
          disruptive.

                    The flooding
deepens,

          its velocity   of water
and light   scooping

the cool
banks,   the outpouring

attracting
          our thought to

                         a space
expanding

               and interrupting.
          Having

               no space
into which   to fall,

     the flow   flows
               apart

and through   itself.
                    Nothing pulls

          at us
like this   shining   water,

          its cycles
and waves   seizing

     the possible,
               its chanting

          pitch
and swell   drowning

                    the sky.
What water

                              understands
            most

is what   gravity
                              demands,

            along with
a willing   cooperation

            of currents
                    or undertows.

    It navigates
                              orbits

around   immoveables,
            preferring

                    the intelligence
of resisting   less.

Filling   space
            with the cloudburst

        of cataracts
                    and cascade,

its voice
            holds   the allure

of where   it has

                        come from,

            the potent   charm
of where

                   it might go.
      A wider

consciousness
               is contemplated.

Intent
            on filling

                  the shape
    of a shape,

            it floods
the mind,   a light

           billowing,
breaking   into

     particles, a like
                 attraction

of each   new
        thought

     integrating
            another.

We imagine   it all,
          resorting   here

to lengthy

                              measures

              of reflection,
thinking

              this design   might
                        carelessly

overtake us,
                    an ephemeral

      caress
                  converging   into

attraction.
                        Nothing

              we say   can
suppress this,   taking

                  us into
      its arms,   pressing

us into   the purpose
                        of its motion,

                              never
doubting   it returns

                    to its beginning.
Two rivers

                    escaping,
the surplus

            brimming,
converging,   their ripple

            and shake
                        altogether

unsure   of this way
        or that,   flooding

            into the surge
                        and torrent,

a downpour
                    overwhelming

            the best
                        of known

intentions.
                    Thinking

                        little,
            except for

the attraction
                    of opposites,

                    we resist
nothing,

                    marvelling
        at the rich   allure,

release
                    of letting go.

THE OCCUPIED MIND

WRITING THAT SNOW IS FALLING

Writing   that snow   is falling

    at the edge   of spring

brings   to mind   new   thoughts

    particular   as particles

blanketing   networks   of white

    branches   or bare   round

buds   anticipating   green   leaves.

    What occupies   the mind

is a vaporish   likeness   bringing

    a disruption   and accumulation,

    an awakening to an intention.

Being   neither   indifferent   nor

steadfast,   the mind   finds   a   way

    to order   an attentive   eloquence.

This reflection   of you   emerges,

   adhering against the unlikely

     ornament of the mind.

Your likeness gathers momentum,

   brimming   the surface

with   its   tenuous   appearance

of appearance.   Into this   mindful

   thinking without thought,

the mind   looks back   on itself.

   A mirror   of   belief

  reflects   briefly while   all

the while thinking   this extension

of thought   inevitably   gives

  rise   to the persistent   heart.

THERE IS NO THOUGHT IN THINKING

There is   no   thought   in thinking

    of you,   this being   neither

common   sense   nor   reason

    that   first   brings to mind

      the moist   breeze

that is you.   Into   this climate

    of thinking   the wayward

mind   is a simple   weather,

bent   on   desire,   disobedient

    and resolute   in its every

appetite,   fixed   on casting

    a small   momentary

doubt into every word, disbelief

    into   every   heart.

OCCUPIED AS IT IS THE MIND

Occupied   as it   is   the mind

    preempts   our   common

intention,   resolved   as it

   is   to roam   seductively

ahead   of its   growing   narrative.

    And   like   a river

filling   its banks,   unable

to hold   in   what   it can   no

longer   carry   forward,   the mind

  will   respond,   inviting

progress,   exceeding   itself,

  discovering   you are   here

after   all,   waiting   patiently

  at the edge   of thought.

IN SPRING A PROFUSION OF BLACKBIRDS

In spring a profusion of blackbirds

    populates the slow progress

of the mind where all thought

    collects, unseen, continually

in motion. As if yearning to be

    everywhere, the dark matter

of the flock is the art of locating

what is not there, without knowing

    exactly what it is or where.

The mind lingers over this puzzle

    of things, probes the latitude

of its being. So it is that thought

    thinks of itself as accretion,

a migration of pent-up directions.

The mind   that loves   to look

    back   on itself,   a mind

that steadfastly   sings   to the heart

    and fills   the empty   body

with thought,   is difficult   to know,

    harder yet to realize.   We wait

for it   to reveal   itself   the way

    hearing   a bird's   song

makes us   search   for   the bird

    itself,   as if   the two

separated   were not to be   believed

    without   knowing   full well

the other   is there,   as if   thinking

    that   alone   will   suffice.

THERE'S THE RHAPSODY OF STARS

There's   the   rhapsody   of   stars

and   then   there's   thinking,

which   often   fails   to bring   about

a pleasing   trajectory   of thought.

Our appreciation   lingers   between

the mind's   disruption

and   its intention   set   in motion.

Just as   each hour   of the day

orbits   and occupies   itself,   the mind

circles   and   then   inhabits

the progress   of its   being.   We take

the position   there is   no   way

of   bringing   this sequence   to light,

nor   in anticipating   its   return.

THE FOOLISH MIND TOSSES

The foolish mind tosses

 and turns in its own breezy

embrace. The soothing mercy

 of its folly is the elusiveness

of knowing it belongs in the know,

 not unlike when a shadow

announces itself through the sun.

   The true constellation

of the mind is of an unwise kind,

  mounting a dialogue that

intersects a recognition of love.

 All the while our heart spins

  this way and that, urging

the whole to agree with its parts.

Our   intimacy   sprawled   across

   the bed   is not   the familiarity

we like   to think   it might be,   nor

   does it   lead   away from   or to

what   passes   between us   as love.

   Yet every   thought   will have

its conviction,   each heart immersed

   within   its   own   re-invention,

entering,   enlarging   our world.

   Preference   is often   given

to those   persuaded   to believe this.

   Nonbelievers   will   try   hard

to carry   it forward,   never   being

   certain   of   its   outcome.

A MIND WITH A MIND OF ITS OWN

A mind with a mind of its own

   assumes the soundless   arc

of a bird in an evening breeze.

   Finding common cause in this,

a resolute heart lingers in the casual

   flight, leans into its shared

escape with swooping birds who

   hiss or howl, hymn or hoot.

   A mind of its own might sing

to all manner of capricious thought,

   whereas the unwavering heart,

willing in devotion, calls out to

desire at every curve, nourishing

   an unquiet welling of uncertainty.

AT THE HEART OF THINGS MEMORY

At   the heart   of things   memory

   will   follow   gravity   when

the dull   weight   of its   misdirection

   leads   us   astray.   The mind,

never   sure   of its   final   bearing,

   will   find   a way   to spin

back   on itself,   not as   another

   way   of thinking   but formed

   in the shape   of its turning.

The information   we have   on this

is contrary.   You   surprise   me   as

   you retreat   in dismay,   knowing

the symmetry   of things   is always

   in danger   of beginning   again.

Like *noise of the pouring river*

the mind lets go, throws spray

like   water's   pulse and hurl.

What's true for the waterfall

is true for the water before its fall,

at the brink   recalls and

recoils, spins and rolls forward

into that fall.   It never runs out,

never loses the weight

of its being, the nervous stuttering

surge of energy at its conversion.

The river   pours, but is always at

the edge, the border   of ordinary

purpose   and extraordinary force.

When   aroused   the agile   mind

    is   a self-portrait   in motion.

It yearns   to speak   with the licence

    of the pleased.   It traces

the margins   of itself,   describing

    a silhouette   of personal

provocation,   a strategy of human

    kindness.   It wants   the heart

to understand   this nourishment

    of thought,   its obedience

to a consuming   appetite. We are

    not perplexed   by this desire,

wanting only what passes   between

    us   to be in   our own   likeness.

SO CONSUMED BY EVERYTHING

So consumed by everything

it might long for, the mind

is intricate true and mischievous.

Its loving attraction

to a willing heart is diverted

by each new intrusion

of thought. Living in the hungry

house of its thinking,

its silent voice is everywhere.

Though ever-present and seldom

heard, it makes the fleeting

truth of things both

improvised in haste as well as

complex in consumption.

LOVE LOST IS A SORROW IN THE HEART

Love lost is a sorrow in the heart,

magnifying in the mind what isn't,

making apparent what is.

Its place in all things escapes us,

is known to be neither widespread

nor contained in a lesser whole.

What we can't retrieve runs through

our lives the way water floods

forward, then falls back on itself.

Putting a distance between lost

and found, the mind is neither here

nor there, revealing not what

it knows but what haunts this love,

wisely undertaken but left behind.

The tranquil mind is no airy

nothing, no orderly

landscape of the heart, but shapes

an uncommon place

for our love, an infinite terrain

without middle or periphery.

The heart well knows the careful

cunning of unseen things

while the mind uncouples every

notion or word as though,

from sensible noun

to wise metaphor, the very enterprise

of thinking this way were also

the unravelling of thought.

THE MIND THAT KNOWS BEST

The   mind   that   knows   best,

knows   what it is   to wake

into   the moment,   that buoyant

stillness   we long for   where

all   thinking   has no   thought.

Whereas   each   memory

arrives   as   a persistent   motion,

coveted   or justly feared

for   its   lasting   burden   upon

our   heart. Your   calming

voice   precedes you   into the room

the way   the thought   of you

in   this   comforting   exchange

hovers   near   to what   happens   next.

IF YOUR VOICE BE READY

If   your   voice   be   ready,

so too   the willing   heart,

uneasy   though   the moral

choice   you value   most   is not

what   your   desire   might   choose

but   what   it frees

itself   to be.   Then worry   not

this flight   of thinking,   cast

in a bright   current   flowing   free.

Each   thought   is a tide

and candid   enterprise   returning

to   an honest   mind

a measure   of its own   reprise,

its own   continuous   change.

SOME THINGS WE CAN IMAGINE

Some   things   we can   imagine

as if   they were   something

else,   assuming   they are

understood   or intimate   enough.

In other   approaches   to thinking,

we   voice our   thoughts

as extensions   of the same   thing,

as if   thought   and language

were part   of a joining   the mind

willingly   explores.   When we

empty   our mind   of such things,

and thinking   moves on,

all metaphor   is lost,   subject to

more   reliable   interpretation.

THE FEVER IN YOUR MIND EVOLVES

The fever   in your mind   evolves

    a dilemma   of intersections,

making   our   passing   thoughts

    hard   pressed   to speak

    clearly   in the language

we know best.   In finding   a way

to overcome   what has   escaped

    our apprehension,   what

brings   us here,   quarrelsome,

    indulgent   to an impatient

        meeting   of minds,

is also   an absence   in progress,

a shedding   skin,   a tangled

    forgetting   refusing   to remember.

THE CARESS OF THINGS WE THINK

The caress   of things   we think

     to be true   is the last

     thing   we know   to be real.

In this way   the opposing   mind

disrupts   in order   to compose,

     disperses   to   absorb,

and doubts   to build   belief.

     Nothing   lasts   beyond

     our thinking.   Nothing lives

beyond   the real   forward   motion

of our thoughts.   All we can know

     is the lasting   touch

of another,   a long   integrity,

 constellating with every embrace.

Thinking   what   the night   might

offer,   your fingers, tunnelling,

will find   me empty,   soft

as thought.   We assume   it's better

not   to say   a word,   uneasy with

the   notion   this   feeling

is more   real   than not.   There is

no mistake   in leaving

things   unsaid   for   the very

last   moment.   And so   it is

the slow   steady   heat   of your

tongue, for all its wandering,

that   has   the   final   say,

that   knows   what   it   knows.

THE CONTRARY MIND ARRIVES

The contrary   mind   arrives

    in a rapid   downpour

    of narrative,   being rival to

the incoming   weather of opposing

views.   We've been   around long

    enough   to know   the mind

behind   each   mind   is a distant

    reflection of   its   opposite.

    We have   faith   our love

will   survive   every   scrutiny,

    it   being   capable of hope

and sincerity,   its daily affirmation

    a prevailing   climate

of wilful   confession   and candour.

Thinking   is   the   daily   breath

of the mind, its matter   the free

uncertainty,   temperature

and velocity   of a breeze   weaving

through   the evening   air.

You come   and go   as you please,

overcoming   all known   resistance,

thinking   it best   not   to resist

too   much   in   return. Knowing

all things   must change,

your   breathing   will   often   fall

off   to nothing,   inertia

or some   other   reason

making   it   impossible   to think.

A SLOW RESTRAINT GIVES RISE

A   slow   restraint   gives   rise

in   the mind   to   opportunity.

Our   longing   arrives   with

forgiveness   and   the   familiar

promise   of   necessity.

The electric   hum   of our thinking

is   complex   enough,   by   turn

simultaneous,   appearing

to   be   inevitable,   advancing

the inescapable.   We think

of   pleasure   as   unavoidable

as the mistaken   belief   there is

always   something   much   more

than   there   really   is.

THE MIND EMPTIED OF ITSELF

The   mind   emptied   of itself

        is   a   complication

    in which one finds what one

is looking for. A paradox of this

    configuration carries with it

the heart   of our thinking,   the way

    an empty   room   is occupied

as soon as   the mind   believes you

    to be   there.   You reluctantly

relinquish this   echo   of ourselves,

this thought trumpeting a lightning

    all night long,   this thunder

emptying   itself   of its   sound

    in the opening   between us.

FIRST LIGHT IN THE MORNING

First   light   in the morning,

    spring   thunder   shaking

the house. The growing expectation

   of our   waking   approaches.

You   call   out   without

   knowing   it's your   voice

      that rouses   you

     from   your   sleep.

Into   our mind   the advancing

      storm   pours

    fear and   anticipation.

Thinking   like this   becomes

the unexpected   lightning of our

    want   and   need.

THE MIND IS A STUBBORN EMPTINESS

The mind is a stubborn   emptiness

  where both love and direction

matter, where the magnetic   pull

  of resolve is hardly   ever far

  from   the overflow of desire.

We think   the mind   will never

  satisfy its capacity or purpose,

will   know   nothing of its reason

nor find its vacant heart wanting.

  Oh, but none of this is new.

In   the morning the light   shapes

  the thunder,   and the light

shakes, taking back what it gives

  no matter how much we resist.

THAT THE LAST OF SNOW IS FALLING

That   the last   of snow   is falling,

   then dissolves,   is not   a part

of its falling   away   but melting

   free,   as we think   about it,

   from   winter's casual   touch.

A comparison   both   alluring and

   distracting,   this love of ours

magnifies   inside   us,   a wary

agreement   that weather   expands

   as if   escaping   somewhere.

Balancing   together   this paradox

   of attraction   and   disturbance,

   the itinerant   order   of things

possesses   its own   pull   of gravity.

Our   thinking   inhabits   its own

space,   until it   moves on.

Even   the morning   rain,

beginning   as snow,   transits

where   the landscape   leaves off.

We think   this   must   be

how   pools   then streams   emerge

from   themselves.   This river

of thought   never   ends,   occupies

more   than   itself.   What comes

to mind   appears   and   runs   on,

strangely   confident that

whatever   overflows   embraces

another   meaning   entirely.

THE MIND REFLECTS ON ITS APPETITE

The mind   reflects   on   its appetite

for love   the way   thought

as we   know it   knows   enough

to satisfy   a sense   of its own

beating   heart.   Being   every

thing   that surrounds it,   the mind

must   resist   the diversion

of   opposites,   the   lost   strategies

of excess.   Now   when   we   wake,

the sheets   pooling   like water

around us,   you want   to know   why

what   feels   this   much   like

separation   is also   what we   miss

most,   and   then   turn   away.

EVERY THOUGHT IS WELL EXPRESSED

Every thought is well expressed

    as picture or description, but

seldom shows a notion how

    the elaboration of a breeze

in the cool morning air becomes

    another breeze in a morning

filled with the thought of you.

What we imagine morning noon

and night is the sensible expansion

    of each embrace. In this way,

what we think longs to lengthen

    what it knows, submits what it

wishes to extend to where nothing

    lingers or remains the same.

IMPATIENT MORNING BIRDS LIGHT

Impatient   morning   birds   light

   as feathers   in our   daily

    thoughts   are restless

enough   to know   what   the mind

   calls   into   question,   which

is   after all   a simple   matter

  of what   swoops   into sight.

The mind   is calm   yet the weather

is anxious   as if someone   has been

   thinking   all   along   how

things   will   suddenly   pass   by,

   or what   startles   birds,

  making   them   sweep   forth

from   the bare trees   into   the mind.

A ROWDY CONFUSION RAINS DOWN

A rowdy   confusion   rains   down.

It occupies   us daily with this

thought   of what-is-not,   giving

rise   to a wary yearning or dismay.

Surely what-is-not   must be

the raucous gossip   of our thinking,

a tempest   of the mind   the mind

would   otherwise   cause   to be

withheld,   or   wisely offered.

All   this is   merely weather

of   another   kind   aligning to

the limits   of what-is,   like rain

falling   then   snowing   then

melting   then   vanishing entirely.

THE MIND STRIPPED BARE OF ITSELF

The mind   stripped   bare   of itself

will find   snow   is melting   on

bare   branches   where   less

is the more   we look for   knowing

the more   we know   is less

than   the green   of spring   buds

emerging   slowly   out of   the snow.

We tell   ourselves   this will

suffice   in a world   silent as

melting,   thinking   this   will   find

the morning's   advancing   light,

in defiance   of the night,   spinning

dissolving   into   the   uncertain

anxious   edge   of   something   new.

WHAT REMAINS OUTSIDE THE KNOT

What remains outside the knot

of ordinary life lies in wait

at the hungry edge of your heart,

beating hard against itself

to be free of itself. You can feel

how the body acquiesces as it

opens wide, then discovers what

the occupied mind promises

will never become, nor ever be.

A familiar notion is set in

motion, swirling like a current

between us. The usual suspects

tumble out of the mind, working

hard to free itself of itself.

WHAT THE WILFUL HEART KNOWS

What   the wilful   heart   knows

    about   love   is   more

like a contrary   climate of thought,

    whereas   the capricious   mind,

arriving like a flood, reaches out in

    the daily   downpour   of living.

Why   this matters,   as compassion

    fades   and   reason   thinks

    of   itself as self- sufficient,

is   a reminder   that weather   enters

    our   thinking   without   form

or purpose,   eluding   the illusion

    of perfection while occupying

the vexing pleasure of expectation.

Trying   not   to think   will comfort

the mind   when it   no longer

wishes   to be willing. Likewise,

hesitation,   waiting   in   the pause

between   trying   and not,   empties

itself   of all   inclination.

At   the window   your   reflection

lingers   where   it   also   waits

within   the glass. This is perceived

like   a river   wavering   against

the stone,   unable   to turn   back

or continue,   slipping   through

by   embracing   the stone,   finding

a release   in its   ready   resistance.

IN THE MOMENT A THOUGHT FAILS

In   the moment   a thought   fails,

   or love flees,   there   is no

room   left   for   there   to be   light.

  Spilling toward   where   the day

overflows,   the light   in   the heart

   is made   darker,   its landscape

   becoming   increasingly   close

to no light   at all. Whether   or not

we   know it   like that, we search

  for a way to think of the night

   as what we see in a figure

slowly   gaining   ground   on itself.

Emptying fields of vanishing points,

   you   appear   out of   nowhere.

The unruly   mind   strays   into

    the room,   its disruption,

wandering out of the cold   sprawl

    and   readiness of the rain.

Though   the rain   knows   no shape

before   it   first   falls,   the mind

    of unruly   weather   swells

    into   a tempest   humming

    with   trembling   and   throb.

When   thinking   interrupts itself,

    the self overcomes all reason,

is   of a mind   to forecast   disorder

at the edge of emergence, the shape

    of which   continuously arrives.

THE ATTENTIVE MIND DAILY LOOKS

The attentive mind daily looks

out of the window where

sunlight divides itself from

the sky. The heart expects this,

saying there can be no thought

of separation, only what

the glass provides and the sum

of the light released through it.

The mind sees and the heart

anticipates. The whole in-between

is unconditional, an argument

clear of absolute certainty

awaiting a momentary kind

of delicious unbroken freedom.

AS LONG AS THIS PASSING MIND

As long as this passing mind

is mindful of its appetite

for love, it finds a way to run on

and on, in equal portions

ephemeral, its thoughts lasting

as the buzz and hum

of a river channelled by its water.

What we wish for most,

we often lose in distraction,

an unexpected tributary of sorts

one can't easily ignore. Sometimes

something will simply offer

more than we bargained for,

leaving behind a surge of buoyancy.

WHATEVER ELSE THE MIND MIGHT WISH

Whatever else the mind might wish

   the heart to be, when love

turns up   explaining everything

   the mind   responds in kind

knowing little of its role inside

  an ever widening relationship.

This whorl and tilt of the mind

counters as a balancing   reflection

within   the far fields of our love.

We see each   degree of intimacy

  exists for good reason, while

  paying   attention to the notion:

the world   as a likeness   measured

  is never   as close   as it appears.

Nothing we know runs on and on

   like   a river,   whereas   this

   curve of brief   desire is not

as nearly far along, nor is its

course what links   us   all together.

   Less   a path where nothing

varies   and   more   again   where

   something   undertaken   soon

   arrives,   this desire is the vital

   course that chronicles the swirl

from first temptation to last elation,

   confirming all intervals between

   are not as near, nor is this love

of ours as far apart as would appear.

IT'S EASY TO FORGET HOW MUCH

It's easy   to forget   how   much

   desire   begins   in   hesitation,

how   many   times   what   can't   be

   certain   lingers   near   in   ambush.

   Occasionally   a wavering   arrives

that   can't   be   quite   unravelled;

a questioning   slips   by   before

   what   isn't   known goes   missing.

And yet,   not   leaving   love   behind,

this   desire   will   circle   cautiously

   around,   its   burning   doubt,

   so   attentive   in   the morning

   light,   sometimes   surprising   us

within   the   pressure   of its need.

Being both wishful and mostly

   unattainable, our longing

    might be irresistible

as   is   daylight   to   its night.

But its craving is a tangled place,

   occupying space as contrary

   as the moon. Enticing and far-

flung yet also intimate   enough,

its readiness   arrives with dawn

   or dusk, inclines towards

an   inverse   hope of faraway

   infinity, making distance

   of   desire, yet snares

the   heart with near   proximity.

INVITED TO REMEMBER ONE THING

Invited   to remember   one thing,

  yet   knowing   another,

  you   say   that   every   new

memory   will   contain   the seeds

  of its opposite. So it must be

  another   scale   of thought,

this   capacity   to occupy   empty

space,   that fills us with confusion.

Our uncertainty is   the difference

  between   the unconscious

mind keeping open all possibilities

  and   how a thought   thinks

of itself   as a   breeze   let   loose

  to contain   everything   in its path.

MINUTES

Different than understanding, memory
    is another being, familiar
at times, solitary, learning to live

    minute by minute.
Nothing quite records her eloquence,
    or captures her bright

versions of history. Our eyes close
    against her radiant lights.
Adapting to the darkness, we picture

    her reflection an image
of what we cannot forget. Translating
    what seems to be known,

each new thought becomes incompatible
    with the confusion of night.
Embracing us, her supply of the past

    is continuously present.
Surely designed with opposites in mind,
    her contradictions undermine

our every word. Rushing into the light
    or darkness, we picture her,
agile as flight in her white dress, speaking

    of loss and gain, her promise
a promise of a promise, foretelling now
    everything is possible.

PROPHESY

Not true this perplexing notion
        of an enduring winter,
but a conscious accumulation,

        concentrating, inviting
a careful growth of snow slowly
        swelling to where even

our years of unrest are cautiously
        multiplied, layered
in a deeper white. Nothing we

        might long for, you say,
emerges without having been here
        before. And this is so

because nothing we might imagine
        reaches out without first
reaching back. Skimming the horizon,

        the purpose of the day
is to bring to mind the night. The sky
        beckons with falling

snow, hesitant, letting itself go, setting
        in motion a prophetic
measure. All these hours and minutes

        will make the difference,
shaping themselves in our minds
        like itinerant weather.

SECONDS

The seconds don't matter. Not so
　　　this new winter sun,
its pale light authentic, embryonic,

　　　holding nothing back.
Our mornings, you see, cut across
　　　this fabric of seeing,

taking the bedroom's measure,
　　　intimate as skin.
Mostly efficient, this thinking is

　　　irrationally curious,
hard at work to wake, rising,
　　　electric as a kiss.

We've had in mind a feverish
　　　beginning, warm blood
persuading the seconds to continue

　　　into minutes, only
to find something wholly different,
　　　more than counting.

What matters most is thinking
　　　without thought. Nothing
else considered, the quick release

　　　of unreason is promptly lost,
though wisely, we've never imagined
　　　each other that way.

PROTOCOLS

Waking to you this way, firing up
           the morning, online,
all of our memories become more

           like brief interventions
filling our heads with a new present.
           Our protocols are saved

in the short term, outstripping what
           we know, made more visible
in the longer term, seasonal as snow.

           The immediate is another
way of seeing what might come next.
           We press down the keys,

stroking the words, intimate intentions
           sent, contemplating
face-saving fictions for another day.

           We anticipate this new
network, where something near
           is not, and close to us

is what is far away. Talk to me now,
           you say, overcome, saying
there's no time like the present,

           nor room to find
ourselves while searching, inventing
           something out of nothing.

ASYMMETRICAL

What isn't balanced is quickly
       countered. Outside, a pattern
decomposes in a snow-filled sky,

       its proportions craving
space for more of what is missing.
       It looks to be a part

of what is not, of what we surely
       long for. Inside, our sense
of things reveals itself, discordant,

       across a line of fluid shapes
without a shape. Nothing we measure
       in our minds omits

its opposite, something of a parallel,
       mirrored, bristling
with possibilities and differences.

       At the first harsh word
we press on through, you in your
       white dress, so different

in the way you walk, setting in slow
       motion, slow motion.
It all changes, you say, in crossing

       the room, your reflection
falling behind itself, never content
       with what lies ahead.

DISGUISES

No horizon is in sight, the flooding
       snow shaping the air.
Its cool silence is faceless, in many

       parts foreign to ordinary
recognition, making counterfeit
       the intention of things.

From the window, this weather
       misleads us. Nothing
in the scene is willing to be seen,

       no thought on display
can be hidden, enticing doubt
       or notions of learned

illusion. Minutes flow by, each
       one pretending to signify
its opposing end. Our argument

       is in favour of endless
familiarity, moment to moment.
       All of which is to say,

little separates one thing from
       the other, we can agree
on that, but this all might be deceit

       of another kind, a feel
of the commonplace, continuous
       enough, and perfect.

SEPARATIONS

We are at our best when least ourselves,
        departing from the fields
of who we are, searching for a stone

        of clarity, a countryside
uncovered. In this guise we inhabit
        a ready light revealing

itself, which is why you say the night
        is a bird that never
comes to rest, an image deceived

        by the open mind
into believing it is somewhere else.
        The meaning of this

is hard to hide in our hands, or set free
        in the sky. The air is filled
with the raw scent of snow. The wind,

        willingly, sets this in
motion, pressing for a miracle, for another
        destination. When night falls,

followed by the first snow, it brings
        with it the reason behind
this metaphor, how it will shape us now

        and tomorrow. What
we hope for matters, and what we know
        is the difference that follows.

ANSWERS

In the confusion, this image of winter
      waking us, impatient, when
we least expect it. Knowing at once

      what the answers
might be, we understand the questions
      better. This is both

a departure and arrival, you say,
      pointing out the light
swelling the horizon. Doubtful when

      the spring might appear,
now clearer descriptions clouding
      the particulars of morning,

we meet in the first melt of the day,
      uniting our uncertainty.
There are dramas we make up,

      and those invented for us,
bright fields of symmetry and difficult,
      ambiguous reflections.

Miracles are given for us to solve
      and share, though nothing like
this might have happened before now,

      nothing in the shape
of this likeness, dispersing, merging,
      a parting and meeting of sorts.

SUCCESSION

The mornings are bright and short.
      But with noon, the wintery
skyline softens, as does the wary mind.

      We make a marriage
of the heart, blessings and vows worthy
      of these briefer days

altering these uneasy rooms. Our love
      is known in weakness
and in strength, our patience now a part

      of what desire brings.
When, as hasty days retrace their steps,
      arriving in the evening

at an end of things, you say it is this
      half-heaven in the light
that gives us what we always wished

      to know. Like weather
welcoming our thoughts, arriving where
      it's learned to land,

this love brings us closer to the closing sky.
      These relentless minutes
and hours emerge unsettled, withdrawing

      from an uncertain
passing, the snow only now showing
      the shape of its hiding.

PROPORTIONS

Most properly celestial, significantly
       terrestrial, the morning
snow lets loose illuminations, rough

      ghosts of stars embracing
essentials of our histories, material
       in their shining moments.

No response to the day can be too
      rational, you say, in this case
a challenging relationship, the divine

      confrontation of reason
and light, growing discreet, then
      weightless in the morning air.

Is this not how we began, impulsively
      mixing an equal share
of need and reconciliation? Might our

      finish then be sincerity,
painting all the bold elaborations of age,
      the carelessness of inhibition?

At this point, confronting the bare air,
      a reworking of the day
emerges on the horizon, falling to us

      to find the proper mix, what
clear *scienza* of beginnings will outlast
      even our most difficult days.

SATURATION

Burdened with snow, this wind has little
         to say in the matter,
believing the snow knows its own mind,

         occupying as it does
an open sky, freely adapting to the space
         all around. The wind

becomes a whirlwind, picking up loose
         ends and burying others.
This is more than we might imagine,

         you say: the wind letting go
sets the trees in motion, a progression
         of locations relocating,

a force giving rise to a new meaning
         for the living snow.
So this notion of the snow arrives

         before the wind, shifting
its thinking to suit the needs of another
         at odds with its prevailing

airborne self. Shaking free, the snow
         extends even farther than
the wind might expect, following a path

         of falling away, relentlessly
releasing what the winter lets go when
         it lets go of everything.

HOURS

Nothing is less necessary,
      these hours, humming
like electric tremors, recursive,

      nesting each one
inside the other. How absurd
      their travels, forming

periods of dense arrival, lingering,
      delayed interludes.
No time is a better sign of wiser

      happenings, a subtle
stillness released, accumulating,
      dismissing all our

raw measures. Today you nearly
      fooled me, letting
loose your hair, disappearing

      into the bedroom light.
But how wonderful to find you
      still here, as if you

never left. Our intimacy, you see,
      takes no time at all,
whereas our distances have rare

      meaning, celebrating
every instant, always at the brink
      of what comes next.

PRIMITIVES OF MEMORY II

The most sensible thing to do
      is to plunge into memory.
There, at least things will be

      tested, overflowing,
without puzzle or sadness,
         never knowing to what

shape we must adhere.
      In no time there will be
a sinew of lingering doubt,

      a hushed story evolving,
unwinding, stroking the curves
      of right and wrong.

The beating heart of all this
      is uncertainty, feeling
like the elegance of abundance,

      apologue of the blind,
or perhaps it's the spiral of falling
      snow, geometric and cold.

The wisdom of seeing less more
      often is not forgotten or lost,
while a thousand hungry starlings,

      hidden behind our eyes,
align themselves in a long
      chattering line, unbroken.

SYMMETRICAL

Who is without reflection, opening
      unlikely likenesses
upon the world? Bringing together

      our similarities, our faces
look back, filling in the symmetries.
      Our midpoint shows

a stillness, not unlike this mirror,
      imitating thought,
self-consciously uncertain, reflexive,

      the mind looking to turn
itself around. We measure these rich
      depictions, together

sorting through coherences, integrating
      this much bigger picture
of head and heart. Our field of vision

      widens, joining us
to vanishing points, concentrating
      this model of being.

Yet nothing stays still for long.
      The true blessing of motion
is in moving away from ourselves,

      releasing the real limits
of our limits, what the mind mistakes
      for our differences.

DAYS

Looking more like amber, losing
      the last of the night,
our bedroom awakens, eased into

      a light used to measure
a fragile longevity. More or less
      subject to the same

motivations, the days begin at rest,
      impatient, awaiting
the next new moments. We find it

      so easy to believe
in a momentum of things, confessing
      to being drawn toward

the art of the possible, full knowing
      its darker peripheries
will sideline us long before we see

      the other side. The days
arrive full of promise and diversity,
      sometimes with unexpected

solitude. They release like sparrows
      escaping into the sky,
calling into question this random

      logic of knowing
what the air lets go, freeing thoughts,
      finding nothing missing.

NEGOTIATION

What brings us closer also sends us away.
We agree to contradiction,
the inconsistent mind pursuing a constant

language of the heart.
Our talk endures in mediation, freeing
revelations and regret.

We welcome confession and defiance
adding to our belief in
the here and now, combining the skill

of matching this with that.
What outcome might we soon expect?
Our conversation is compliant

in this way, its light adapting to the very
shape of things. We seldom
know the ending. It's in the patterns,

you say, that radiant art
of substitution we understand the least.
A proximate cause holds

together these metaphors. As always,
one thing leads to another,
though little is foreseen. This insight

appears conclusive, a brief
result of passing through this medium,
our union, this intimacy.

EMANATION

The leaves, the rain, the things we know
      without thinking.
We'll walk again, down toward the water,

      talking (morning
as usual beginning to flow), and continue
      past the river, spreading

east, the sandy path disintegrating, yellow
      grass at our knees.
Soon we'll come to a source, where things

      we know without
thinking – the disagreement of the gulls,
      the routine of the waves –

release the energetic shape of their being.
      This is where it all can
begin, you say, the enthusiasm of belief,

      a conscious equilibrium
of the present having little in common
      with any real philosophy.

Rising and falling in time, this consistency
      of motive becomes a flood
of adaptation. What might come next?

      What final understanding
is intended, is ours to know, without clear
      cause or emanation?

HYMENEAL

When the mind thinks of itself, there is
      no conscious rhythm,
nothing in our thought for us to reason,

      no pulse persuading
or enticing us to confess or reconcile.
      In the heart of its

cadence, thought sings of itself, much
      as the splintering
wind stirs its abundance, lifting spring

      skies and harbour
birds alike. A marriage of sorts, longed
      for in the personal terrain,

encounters this thinking. Its persuasion
      is a union in progress,
transiting to a place desired most in this

      agile landscape.
Shifting locations from beginning to end,
      we wake into this

new thought, much as we dream of its
      arrival in our sleep.
The mind permits itself to find a partner

      in this contradiction.
The mind emerges out of itself, freewheeling,
      continuously apparent.

INTIMACY

No one knows when it begins, history
        having little weight in
the matter. What will happen, happens,

        here in our thinking,
known or imagined, closer to fiction,
        a wise uncertainty.

Our story, you say, is more than that,
        more than we can say,
defiantly intimate, occasionally at odds.

        Being next to, close to,
together, we begin where each other
        leaves off. There is no

confusion in this proximity, awaking
        to each other's thoughts.
We sleep late when we can, fitfully,

        again in the afternoons.
The closer we are, the outside world
        converges. Inside, the sunlit

windows are glowing, glazing to a glassy
        reflection, doggedly
sheer, oddly artificial. Finding this light

        is a habit we daily follow,
sometimes arriving late, and long before
        we know it to be here.

LIGHTNING

Some things are simple: as air is, as
       the rain, as silver is as
clear as air and rain, as light is before

       finding itself, recoiling
in gravity, designed to give shape to
       the air, as honest as

falling rain is, enlightening, as air is
       disturbing, dissolving.
In that place where our love is, you say,

       words fall like rain.
No one can live inside that uncertainty.
       Rain leaves the sky.

The light leaves the rain. Our words
       tumble out, slick as silver,
a line of light we reach out to pass on,

       appearing out of nothing,
complex as a glance. The sky opens up
       to the clear air, solid as

the mark we know to be there. Some
       things are simple as this,
this light, familiar as breath, urging us on.

       Some things make
more of a difference, burning through air,
       an unthinkable scar.

QUIET

We lie in the cool shade of the tree.
There is nothing here
we haven't heard before, the cicada

singing an insistent
buzz, invisible, high in the thinnest
branch. Then, a silence.

The song won't end if we don't wish it,
you say, waiting for
its beginning to begin again, imagining

what it would be like if it
had no end, if the joining of one end
to the other was unbroken.

That might be too much like love, too
close to the idea of love,
the hum of it in our heads, murmur

of heat, hunger in between.
It is this ending and not this beginning
that troubles us most.

Second by second the cicada suspends
what it knows, what it
wants to say in its pitch-perfect song.

The air is quiet, unsure
of what has gone missing, impossible
to retrieve it, no matter what.

GRIEF

The end of the day takes into account
       what will escape
our grasp, an instant with an' hour

       of its own, so haunted by
the weariest of feeling, disappearing,
       only to reappear

when we least expect it. There are no
       directions for this,
though soon enough we'll find it,

       weightless as air, how
it spirals upwards, difficult as starlight,
       claiming a severe dignity.

Never mind, you say, each memory
       will embrace us willingly.
Someone will notice the birds

       in the evening, descending
in perfect order, one by one, or locked
       into smaller flocks.

Others will believe what they want to,
       explaining a flight
of ghosts, migratory, expressing what

       is celestial to hold.
What we know of grief is a shadow,
       empty in our arms.

ARRIVAL

An orderly end to the day pours out
       of the street. Emptiness,
you say, first appears as a fading

       confusion. Clarity
of feeling is overrated, I say, hoping
       to smooth our muddle

of *melancholia* (a blue devil
       as it's affectionately known)
and welcome quiet reflection. Threads

       of thinking puzzle
along, heartsick and downhearted
       at the thought of being

in the dumps. Some things stay with us
       so long they take on
a direction all their own, are so often

       overwhelming it's hard
to make out each measure of meaning.
       Nothing is the same

after being down so long. This lengthy
       way around comes
to greet us all, sooner or later:

       we look out as far as we can,
never sure we'll arrive before
       knowing we're already there.

PLANETARY

Sensible as air, these planets,
   roaming the sky, weaving
fluid shine and radiant sideswipe.

  Soundlessly migrating
together, they flourish distractions,
   presenting themselves wary.

Their markings chase the night's
   arrival, circular lines
of shade and nuance, apparition

  and progression forwarded
to a tranquil destination. They are
  more than one or many,

you say, a problem complicating
   things, disguising what
we long to better understand.

  Our devotion to finding
a reason for everything knows
   no limits, our memories

coming up against the seeds
   of galaxies. Imagination lets
loose where this shape of thinking

  appears, the heavens
above so much more than mere
   concentration of harmonies.

Willing grace upon us, memory
            intrudes, making known
its promising signs and prophetic

            uncommon ways.
What is most surprising is never
            what you might expect,

but the pull of things will take over,
            directing the sun
to find its rest, bringing the night

            to a disappearing sky.
Shall we dream again, or not?
            Or see this life differently,

like love, gathering intensity,
            indistinguishable from light?
Above us the sky will be freed

            of its bearing, a necessary
momentum flying into our narrative.
            Heavens will shift.

The night's horizon, curving, emerging
            out of itself, will lean
into its own constellations, whereas

            our navigation through
this firmament is careful not to trust
            the illusion of direction.

CONTINUUM

As we are, our walk along this path
      is much like the visible
stars set in motion, not for the present

      but for the longer term.
Not unlike our continuing memory
      of things, you say,

yet there is something to be said
      for saving time, leaving
nothing behind, suspended, joining

      the inextinguishable.
We bear witness to how things alter,
      lose their way or return.

Even as the evening closes, concentric,
      it becomes a bonfire
of change. Not quite so new to this,

      we can forget more than
we might recall, our orbits tethered.
      We kiss faithfully,

pressed against the other, haunted, our
      fear of continuous nights
imperfectly fleeting, knowing well

      that last time we looked up,
we mistook this expanding sphere
      for a much shorter pause.

CONFLAGRATION

This simmering heat, shimmering
    in the air, poses a mystery,
bringing a disorderly breakup to

    an orderly arrangement
of flocking birds. It's a relationship
    on the brink, you say,

a reflection of the climate changing,
    migrating closer to us.
Now we've changed too, an unlikely

    transformation, fitting
together with what happens in the heat.
    This intensity does not

think of itself in motion, though we are
    thinking of it now, how bright
it has become. In a minute that has

    no movement, it is
the final pulse of the moment, merely
    breathing its last.

The birdless sky, combusting, ablaze
    contains what it consumes.
So we are held in the likeness of this

    impossible embrace,
a stillness, burning through, this notion
    of what things are.

AFTERLIFE

We'll try to get this right, you say, paying
      close attention to the elements
like rustling leaves or the wet, timid earth.

      As we go forward, it must be
in our minds, wary of the senses, nervous
      of what is seen or understood.

The first time you see impossibilities
      mounting, think of them
as giving up the darker ground, the last,

      lasting concentrations of will.
Precarious, invoking these landscapes,
      the difficult terrains emerge.

The world is made of mountains made
      of minutes and hours
converging like eloquent calculations

      of the incomprehensible.
We enter a dream, following a shadow
      without form, shapeless as

the close air we breathe. We go forward,
      in our minds a humming
hypnotic sound filling the emptying sky.

      All we know of our thinking
is what we can know of its sudden release,
      a giving or taking of everything.

CAUSE

Something rational in the air, a cloud
     or spring seeds drifting
into view, transforming. You suspect

     it might be close to reason,
shaping what explains us. Looking
     into it, our conversation

quickens, willing us to witness all that
     is beginning. It's nothing
but motive or cause, you say, breathing

     in the impossible, the unwise.
If we are its reason, you will wonder
     how a doubting word

can steal away what we know as sensible.
     The effect of this is neither
right nor wrong. It finds us willing, full

     of blessings for the fallen,
joy for the newly claimed. It finds an end
     to a conversation, ready

now to unravel the loss of hours and days,
     to find a return to a patient
abstraction. This marriage of minds complains

     at the edge of the day, coming
closer to a triumph of wills, the last reminder
     of any and all misgivings.

EFFECT

A moon is wisely particular, susceptible
          to wider interpretations,
its slow transit by the hour persevering,

          expressive, releasing into stars
nightly repetitions of itself. Open the sky
          and there it is, continuously

present, persistent: the result of its glow
          entering the bedroom,
so bright in places it might be day, you

          alone wishing it could be
the reason for our illumination. The error
          we make is in thinking

we live in this light, the consequence
          of questions and answers
shaking at the edge of a darkness we see.

          It's a confusion of proximities,
you say, so near to each other we can
          make a puzzle of distances.

We recognize our love as this outcome
          of another place. Like pieces
of a different light, it begins and ends

          in this misunderstanding,
something we might see, or a soft voice
          repeating what can't be true.

BEFORE

A ribboning sky, converging, greets
       the evening, laughing.
This effortless harmony, you say,

       has everything to do
with showing what attracts us now.
       Verging on more moon,

more stars, more of night is calling
       out to us. We can talk
about growing expectations, yearning

       for more direction.
Our shadows are long and stretched
       into the far horizon.

In the setting sun flocks of birds disrupt
       the air, their sudden turning
perhaps a language of anticipation.

       We are more than
familiar with this ongoing conversation:
       questions without answers

asking questions. What have we been
       thinking all this time?
All minutes are unbroken now, your face

       incandescent, the last
of the light singing of continuous lives,
       the sky farther than we think.

AFTER

The evening light swirls and eddies,
      stirring heaven's cunning
fabric, witnessing the sky's conversion,

      measuring itself against
darker pools. Its fluid surface is full
      of spirits, slowly recalling

the night. For a long time we look up,
      our breathing probing
the crisp air. The sun's fading light

      is a sinuous landscape
flooding us with stories, anticipating
      the coming star-years.

No mistake, you say, there are reasons
      for everything, some
more irresistible, amorphous than others.

      Take our love, spinning
its hungry rituals, repeating itself, always
      about to reappear. Nothing

explains its clear truth, its darker thought
      in this constant motion.
We fall into the current of its embrace,

      hardly noticing what
escapes our grasp, this infinite turning,
      this velocity of our longing.

CONVERSATION

These words are distractions, minutes
    escaping our breath,
their meaning eluding us, flying high

    in the air, falling to earth.
Their syntax haunts our conversations,
    finding new orders

of belief, persuading us how wrong
    we are to forsake them.
Words are feelings that we see, you say,

    becoming what thoughts become.
Nothing perplexes us more, or alters what
    we might have thought

from what we do not know. Our thinking
    is the evening's cipher,
its noon a parable of light. The wedding

    of the whirling morning
birds, slipping free, turns us from the night
    into the coming day.

Hunting the missing, the incomprehensible,
    these words are freed,
filtering the joy of the all-seeing heart.

    Contained in this shape,
their only way forward is an old precision,
    the fluency of delight.

UNSPOKEN

We are wedded to these minutes, save
    for this day, slipping away,
collecting itself, clearing a path

    to the unruly overture of night.
The unspoken law of our desire skims
    between us, distracted,

winging fast as a Mediterranean wind,
    at first isometric, then
haphazard, thermal, deliberate in its

    windswept world. Far better
than memory this is, brighter than moon's
    light, alphabet of flight.

Our desire is welcoming, promising
    as swallows to us (imagining
their rising), impossibly complex, confidently

    elusive. How easily
the mind liberates this picture. Flocking
    to horizons, astonished

at the crossing of time, all this invokes
    an improbable calm
between us, pressing ourselves against

    the whole, air currents
firmly in favour of the idea of desire,
    swelling with disorder.

UNSAYABLE

Our unspoken words, harrowing,
      in a cooling wind they climb
into the flesh. Unlike what we promise

      each other, we wonder
what could be another way of saying
      what we don't. Famously

silent, we never ask the question,
      or change our riddled ways.
Salutations to an attenuation of sound,

      to the slower intention
of hum and will, crossing over to solitude.
      There, you see it

there, gathering an attentive ear,
      constellating the mischief
of an incidental life. What we hold in

      our open arms either is
unsayable or is too persuasive
      to accommodate, too intimate

to measure. The voice presents itself, yes,
      apparently willing,
now moving into its opposite. Desire

      seeds itself in this way.
The wind carries us far enough, a grand
      possibility, dispersed.

PERMUTATIONS

Our line of thinking is discrete, linking
      us together, living
all these years, finding the raw order

      of things discontinuous,
not always knowing what comes next.
      Mornings we arrange

what suits us best, successions of coming
      and going, assenting
to the affection of days, the exhaustion

      of evenings into the dark.
Our longevity, you say, might not reconcile
      what is slipping away.

Whatever it is, today the quarrel has gone
      out of us, releasing us
as we talk, into an intimacy we barely

      know. Surely this design
matters more than we like to think.
      Its alphabet is new to our love,

a kind of perpetual motion, unorthodox,
      perplexing, making sense
of our every sense. Trying harder,

      we renounce what has no future.
We confess to whatever brings absolution,
      whatever carries the day.

PRIMITIVES OF MEMORY IV

Having seen the incomprehensible,
        silently taking flight,
the closing sky is fractious

        this far along in the long fall.
All symptoms are ripe: a fleeting
        restlessness, shorter breaths

repeating, exhausting the light,
        diffusing through the air
like newly visible rumours,

        promising all that is promised.
This memory is neither true
        nor hypothetical, integrating

peacefully, though nothing here
        can tell us what to say
or do, the calm pleasure of simple

        facts and fictions
carefully revealed. In the end
        our goal is to be converted

to what can't be reconciled,
        to find a perfect way out
of our dream, fully knowing

        whatever happens now
happens only once before giving
        in to a careless mystery.

COMBINATIONS

Morning in the house, before our
        thinking grows invisible.
Outside, the season awakes,

        the window an autumn
light diagnosing the sun, a yellow
        skin disguised as parchment.

These are the days that come to us,
        simple remedies, hard
to come by. The order of their seconds,

        minutes, hours, no longer
matter. New solutions have taken
        over, transmitting time

in double time, restlessly therapeutic,
        flourishing. This renewal
of the day is loosely knit, a necessary

        conversation asking
after our happiness, intimacy, mysteries.
        The heart has a way

of asking what is unlikely to be
        answered, what
fabrication is composed, combining

        much that is opposite.
With this in mind, you say, all possibilities
        are possible.

ENDURANCE

A low hum follows us into the night,
        a sound so elaborate,
so symmetrical, it sounds to be another

        way of speaking.
It is the voice we hear at the cloud end
        of the day, a sweet

readiness of language, the pleasure
        of breathing, deliberate.
At this late hour there is no one else

        to hear what we hear,
this voice asking after the endurance,
        the ambitions of love.

There is the promise of knowing
        the voice we hear,
the air like a restless narrative carrying

        the opposite of sound.
It is a distraction from another way
        of hearing, the voice

divorced from itself, thinking its own
        true self fulfilled.
It sounds like the persistence of memory,

        you say, prolonging
what we face in the stillness of the hour,
        the continuing mind.

AURORA

Everything comes together, having light.
    What happens to us
is far from ordinary, beginning by falling

    out of the sky, thinking
ourselves open to interpretation, pushing
    against the latitudes.

Here, on the evening side of the inlet,
    birds are accelerating
into the air. Seconds later, the rising mist

    wraps the forest
into shadow. We circumvent the angle
    of the horizon. Our reason

for being, you say, is everything about
    being in place, a quickening
circle, flying into a darkness only minutes

    away from its beginning
and end. What matters is everything
    that comes forth, displacing

an interval charged by reflection,
    proximate to the earth's curve.
Our contemplation is mesmeric, magnetic,

    the sure allegiance of light
raining down, welcoming the distances,
    perfectly placed.

COMFORTING

When morning comes, I'll comfort you,
     though not a comfort made
in anxious haste, nor comfort bred to be

     both practical and wise,
but comfort in the morning made, speaking
     everything and all to you.

When morning comes, I'll comfort you,
     yet holding nothing back,
holding close what draws us wishing for

     each touch, that touch we
cannot make without us being as we are.
     When morning comes,

have no fear of shadows, the sense of them
     too real to imagine, and
more than they can be. I'll comfort you

     when comfort comes, lying
still, as being motionless can will our
     thinking through this world.

Without end, it is, this wonder at what
     changes every hour.
Even now, our brief life here is settled

     in this morning's light, where
fresh symmetries lie waiting, ready to make
     sense of all that we can know.

MULTITUDE

The mind, the mind has a place for it,
  the multitude of seasons
possessing the years, the mountains

  of weeks and months, even
the seconds disguised as yellow-winged
  birds small enough to flock

in dozens and dozens, in and out
  of the willow trees. That place
you say, has never been simple, never

  what we might expect,
though the mind will see what it wills,
  that razor edge between

itself and the landscape trapped inside.
  Yet the willows are empty,
or perhaps they merely are ready to empty

  one idea for another,
a design of things always starting over.
  This is when we begin

to understand: the mind has a way
  of refusing to believe
what it sees, of multiplying the repetition

  of one flight after another,
emerging from its lone self into
  the sensible reason of the many.

PATIENCE

Believing everything you have to say
    is like the virtue of one
becoming the thorn of another, or another

    way of saying there is
everything to fear in the habit of saying
    nothing. Morning, noon

and night, our patience is without limits,
    is of the right consistency,
will always say what does not wish

    to be heard.
This composure of ours finds its place
    inside a calm restraint,

pressing us into its sharper pressure.
    The day begins, you say,
within a certain expectation, at its prickly

    edge an attraction
to an uncertainty, how belief gathers
    together what we know

we don't know. At the end of the day
    there is always room
for the given. Getting it right is a test

    we set ourselves, briefly
impatient with the overflow, content
    with all remaining options.

The trees, the nervous trees, the impatient
     leaves are pushing against
the constant pull of a centre yearning for its

     border. Finches are flamboyant,
their yellow stripes more vivid than ever,
     more so than magpies

in winter, where black on white will find
     no limit, no definition.
Out of these farthest points they emerge,

     flying into an understanding
of proximity, uncertain whether the eye
     will favour their midpoint

or periphery. For us, this much is true:
     no distance is so
unsettling as the time it takes to go

     through it. We navigate
dark forests of human measure, offering
     the particular, the motionless,

appearing for all the world like opening
     a new direction. You say
this also might be a fluid point of view:

     in the place of the whole,
an idea compressed, surrendering its edge,
     releasing into empty space.

TRAJECTORY

This shape of the air is not the shape
      of the bird, but the shape
of the air inside it. Sensing the shape

      and thought of this,
the bird yearns to think of itself as the air,
      spreading its wings in

all directions, filling empty distances.
      In the arc of their hunting,
flying solo or flying as a flock, how birds

      in the air gather birds
together is simply another way of thinking.
      We long to be taken into

their modest range, their marriage of rise
      and subside, their appetite
for elusive flight. Thinking these things

      is the pleasure of knowing
what design brings to intention, how one
      contour completes another,

competes against the next. The pull, pull
      of the air around us curves
around us. We launch ourselves into it,

      making the most of who
we were, filling in what we've become,
      and what emerges next.

SLEEPING

A desire of night is a peaceful day, much like
    you sleeping into the morning,
so still, so composed no one can see or know

    you are here. There is nothing
to wish for, neither the night's brief bloom
    nor its cold air sweeping away

the moon's glare. Yet we know this flash
    of time will pass us by
unnoticed: something turns to nothing, brings

    forth the invisible, turning away
from an unfinished world. What happens
    is a trace of our vanishing hours,

stretched out, motionless, trailing the scents
    of heaven, the wheeling stars
of a firmament hidden in the near horizon.

    Our unspoken promise is always
the nourishment of the night, the sum of the day.
    You say we need nothing else

in a time when there is nothing else to need.
    We begin to suspect
its measure is a shadow in a shadow, keeping

    pace with the pressing
light, never sure what finds its way back to us,
    nor what will come to pass.

RESONANCE

It's impossible to think of you, and not
        think of longing for your
touch. We set in motion ideas like these,

        not unlike the way
summer heat shimmers or the impatient
        night arrives like a tide.

In the spaces between us, everything
        is silent, a light-filled
wave of memory rolling back on itself.

        The last word is never
the last, you say, but a force finding its
        way to the next, prolonging

a continuous energy of its own. This is
        how we think of things,
surfacing somewhere between translation

        and imitation, finding what
makes sense, what next promises to leave
        nothing to chance. It would be

impossible to think otherwise, were it
        not for the sly pleasure
of learning that silence is the very first

        invention of sound,
a heartbeat, resonant, never confusing
        the need of one over the other.

FLYING

The path we take is a question on the way
             to arrival, a sweet problem
of meaning riding the ragged air.

             Sometimes the intention of what
we ask is never what we thought it
             might be. There are no

limits to this confusion. In the blue sky
             of our thinking, this might be
a sign of the other side of love. Someone

             will invent the reason why
this is so. Others will say this is the way
             of thinking, the opposite

of invention, what we long to know when
             asking what to think next.
An idea flies out and doesn't come back,

             a gift breaking free of itself,
caring only to soar beyond what it thought
             might be true, what at last it might

know of itself. This is not love wishing
             to be somewhere it was not
meant to be, though we will think it so.

             Something will tell us there
is more to this than what we intended,
             what is clearly unexpected.

PRIMITIVES OF MEMORY V

The pleasure of memory attracts,
        an appeal of pushing against
the grain, its constant flight unable

        to begin on its own, or bring
itself to an end. Its presence
        presents itself, a coming out

of sorts, something always
        mysterious, half-dark, insensible.
No one can see it happening,

        eyes shut, though its unfinished
course is open ended, adapting
        to a means of slipping free.

All memory emerges out of itself,
        in dreams like celestial bodies
full of wishful thinking, broad

        as nighttime, reconceived.
Tonight the restless stars
        will howl over something more

than the skies pulling apart,
        fresh openings ready to transform
the light of day. This memory is never

        the end of things, but quite
the opposite, a beginning not one
        of us is capable of stopping.

TRACE

Knowing something is in the air,
      the horizon promises
a line of escape. We are this close to one

      of its truths, the dark flocks
of wind-bent birds lining up the luminous
      day. Another truth

forms a conversation, not knowing that
      reflection in the window
is yours, or the truth that is the thread

      of our words is pouring
through the trees. Something soon will
      overwhelm us, you say,

wondering if this is something we'll
      survive, or find ourselves
newly transplanted, misplaced, replaced.

      This line of thought
holds us for a minute, an hour, keeps us
      thinking that radiance

does not withhold itself, is not conscious
      of itself, but follows
a trajectory against its light. The birds

      do not sing; the leaves
do not move against themselves. Everything
      is ready, willing.

CROSSROADS

There would be everything to gain
      if our desire knew which
road to take, leaving behind these

      darker hours, at the heart
of which the uncertain heart finds
      itself without direction,

its needs outside the reach of light.
      Doubt is the weakness
of this desire, its strength a weakness

      for bringing to a head
what can't be overlooked. Desire
      in this is fast and slow,

longer than we can remember, waiting
      for us like an unfinished
task or path not taken. Here is no ease

      of access or escape, knowing
full well it will intersect our thoughts,
      and find a way to undertake

the pleasure of its need. Love will know
      the answer. Love insists
on something other than the separation

      of here and there, curious
to find all distances collapse, nourishing
      the hope of more to come.

QUESTIONS

Hesitant at what the future might be,
    the story of the night
flees from itself, immanent and vital.

    We ask what element, relocating
to morning, keeping its purpose withheld,
    is so ready to withdraw

at a moment's notice? We respond
    by pushing back against this,
pulling things together, occupied as we

    are with questions. Could this
be a subtle error of judgment, ill-timed,
    recreated in the dark,

unforeseen and irresistibly complex?
    Hard to know what is, what
could be, or comes next. All our answers

    ride the tips of our tongues,
persuading the daylight to materialize,
    a rhetoric resolved to emerge

out of nothing. This bright fashioning
    is in our narrative, daily
revealing itself, having served our brief

    moment of transition,
yet wary, suddenly finding you missing
    before the light returns.

SCIENCE

Because we will have walked
        a long way, and because
I know you'll be here at the end,

        we can let this hour
and distance collapse around us.
        The old physics of love

is a mystery, a science of matter,
        its motion embalming us
inside each other. Nothing behaves

        outside of our reason,
before coming back to haunt us.
        The principles are sound.

Your heart inside my head
        is an equation of calming
light, a warren of quiet eloquence

        pushing against what
the future might bring. Whatever
        might happen, happens

because we live and breathe inside
        this brief certainty of fractions,
the chemistries of our thought.

        We can believe everything
is possible, even in our harsh need,
        knowing nothing more.

QUARREL

The argument we nurture is carried
        along like a river, nightly
closer to you, closer to me, surfacing

        now at a singular pace.
What we know of it is a broad course
        randomly crawling,

brimming to the moveable challenge
        of shores, pulling us along
in its flow, waters a tangle of branches

        and weeds. From side to side
we reason with and contain its width,
        the why of our discontent

passed along in a dark pouring forth.
        It's ours to have and to hold,
this narrative of its running, something

        to hear, something to see.
At the heart of the matter is a mindful
        flood gathering up all sense,

making necessity a virtue, forgiveness
        a longer curve of memory.
Pray now in this forgetful night, you say.

        We suffer enough in judgment
of our days, like wise fools in the current,
        fearful of the light.

SPIRITS

Some are content to roam the house
        like ribbons of light sifting
the air, transforming rooms. Some are

        content to remain unknown
and hidden, less than they were, more
        than they could be. So we

might better know their hearts, taking on
        the look of spirits too long
contained, their bodies wear the clarity

        of white on white. Though
unsettling in their presence, there is
        little here to surprise.

Buoyant in the wisdom of Plato's ghost,
        knowing what is
is a perfect language we cannot speak,

        a trying suspicion
of belief without resolution. What then
        might we say with certainty

is ours to know? An idea of you alone,
        or moonlight crossing the room?
This measure of thinking thought

        through becomes
but an apparition of its self, the mystery
        of needing to know what is.

VOICES

Our need is the persistence of memory,
       a random necessity,
weightless, mushrooming, its hum

       and sizzle like spring lightning
caressing the logic of what the air
       lets go. What we value

most about memory is knowing what
       comes next, the orderly
intention of one part, forsaken, leading

       to another. We keep faith
with this singleness of mind, this act
       of inclination made

over in the image of what once was.
       When it strikes, each flash
of light is a path of optimism, uncertain

       of its way, its watery hissing
mesmerizing, erratic. All the seconds
       fragment, and matter more.

We add them under our breath, counting
       on counting to connect us
with what keeps us apart. The waves

       of thunder are not at all what
we expect, appearing out of nowhere,
       breaking inside us like voices.

DESTINATION

Calm is this night, our gentle love
        now something like
a meeting place, somewhere to go

        in slow motion.
Roaming through the sheets, we are
        altogether ourselves, our

merging of wills answering each touch.
        Hardly a minute goes by
without thinking this is more than

        somewhere to be. Arriving
here, appearing early or late, is unlike
        any destination, being neither

first nor last in love, a place of both
        reasoning and remedy.
What then will heaven make of love?

        Everything. We cannot say
this mindful notion is foreign to our heart,
        a desire that envelopes us.

Together we acknowledge something
        separate from ourselves.
Set in motion, the night reveals its

        solitude, a dark abundance
quickening, filling a silence wisely
        loved and falsely held apart.

TESTIMONY

The evidence builds to a confession
        casting light on the next
world, finding intimacies of voice.

        Lost or found, it might be
just that simple, not unlike greeting
        the coming of day after

the going of night. Nothing holds
        together like this meeting
of opposites, whether a forest bent

        back against the stretching
wind, or rising waters knowing what
        direction to flow, flowing

this way against the rapids and eddies
        flooding in return. Nothing
is ever lost, whether in moving apart

        or bringing together again.
The thing we most wish to find doesn't
        lose itself in our words

but remains a fluid, unbroken presence.
        The continuous shadows
of the sycamores fall away from the heave

        and flow of the river, spirited
testimony in a slipping free and infinite,
        long-living eloquence.

PENTIMENTI

The end of night throws off its last
        streaming shadow, a black
polishing of the sky, moon-touched,

        vanishing into the face
of morning. Light streaks our bedroom
        walls, uncovering the painting

of you in your luminous white dress.
        The mind reconsiders
itself, searches deeper again, revealing

        where it came from, finding
yet another version of itself, perhaps
        in a painting or recurring

pattern piecing together the facts.
        Of course, the facts
are never what they seem, never what

        they were meant to be.
Their hidden details are best discovered
        in the first person plural,

our two voices exposed, united as one,
        disguised as another.
A truly novel integration and confession,

        so much more than what
we admit to in our longer years, pulling
        together our opposing views.

MINUTES

What disappears, what is left behind,
         instinctively returns
to its contiguous parts. We are neither

         wholly changed nor entirely
the same in its measure. And yet nothing
         escapes this persistent

image of you wistfully crossing the room.
         The pleasure we know
is in watching what is seen, this reflection

         of you so very close,
so far from everything. Elusive as the flow
         of water, each new minute

swirls and eddies, repeats in its array.
         Thinking this way models
our love: like liquid purpose, it drives

         all occasions, a sure
rectitude of water's flooding ways.
         Whatever is lost the mind

will find, though perplexing and difficult
         to know what new order
it will bring to this aggregate of thinking.

         Every thought is lasting.
Our faces radiant. A quiet breathing returns.
         The invisible awaits us.